S

Sh...

ANJANA CHATTERJEE   ILLUSTRATED BY J...

CONSULTATION BY

RUTH BULL, BSc (HONS), PGCE, MA (ED)

QED

Quarto is the authority on a wide range of topics.

Quarto educates, entertains and enriches the lives of our readers—enthusiasts and lovers of hands-on living.

www.quartoknows.com

Author: Anjana Chatterjee
Consultant: Ruth Bull, BSc (HONS), PGCE, MA (ED)
Designers: emojo design and Victoria Kimonidou
Illustrator: Jo Samways
Editors: Claire Watts and Ellie Brough

© 2018 Quarto Publishing plc
First Published in 2018 by QED Publishing,
an imprint of The Quarto Group.
The Old Brewery, 6 Blundell Street,
London N7 9BH, United Kingdom.
T (0)20 7700 6700 F (0)20 7700 8066
www.QuartoKnows.com

A catalogue record for this book is available from the British Library.

ISBN 978 1 78493 935 9

9 8 7 6 5 4 3 2 1

Manufactured in DongGuan, China TL102017

MIX
Paper from
responsible sources
FSC® C104723

FSC
www.fsc.org

Hello, my name is Pango. I'm a pangolin and I love maths! I'll be your guide to becoming a maths master!

CONTENTS

HOW TO USE THE BOOKS IN THIS SERIES

The four books in Year 1 of the Master Maths series focus on the main strands of the curriculum but using the leading Singapore maths approach. This method involves teaching children to think and explain mathematically, with an emphasis on problem solving, focusing on the following three-step approach:

1 Concrete

Children engage in hands-on learning activities using concrete objects such as counters, cubes, dice, paper clips or buttons. For example, children might add 4 cubes and 3 cubes together.

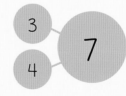

2 Pictorial

Children draw pictorial representations of mathematical concepts. For example, children might draw a number bond diagram showing that 3 and 4 together make 7.

3 Abstract

Children can then move on to solving mathematical problems in an abstract way by using numbers and symbols. Once children understand that 3 and 4 make 7 when they are added together, they can use the abstract method to record it.

$$3 + 4 = 7$$

Each unit of the book begins with a question or statement that encourages children to begin thinking about a new mathematical concept. This is followed by visual explanations and hands-on activities that lead children to a deep conceptual understanding. Children should repeat and vary the activities and be encouraged to revisit earlier sections to seek clarification and to deepen their understanding. You will find extension activities and further instruction in the Parent and Teacher Guidance sections.

When we talk about the **shape** of something, we are talking about the way it fills space.

We can use describing words to talk about the shape of something.

What is a shape?

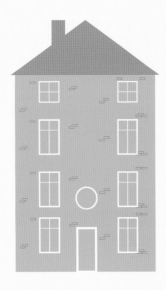

This house is **tall**.
The shape of it is tall.

This house is **short**.
The shape of it is short.

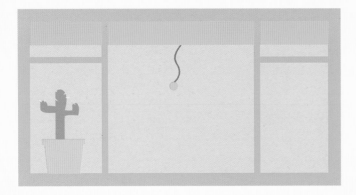

This window is **wide**.
The shape of it is wide.

This window is **narrow**.
The shape of it is narrow.

VOCABULARY: shape, tall, short, wide, narrow

SHAPE NAMES

Some shapes have special names.
Do you know what these shapes are called?

These shapes are called **circles**.
Look at the circles.
What is the same about all of them?

SIDES AND CORNERS

Can you name these shapes?

These shapes are called **squares**.

Look at the square.
Each edge of the square is called a **side**.
Two sides meet at a **vertex**.
How many **vertices** does a square have?
How many sides does a square have?
Look at the sides.
Are they all the same length or
are they all different?

Can you say how a square is different from a circle?

vertex

side

TRY THIS:

Look around you. Can you find some objects that
are shaped like a circle? Can you find some objects
that are shaped like a square?

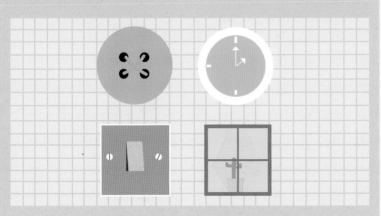

PARENT AND TEACHER GUIDANCE

- Circles are the easiest shapes for children to spot around your home or classroom. Get them started by pointing out clock faces and buttons.

- For squares, point out windows, sticky notes or cheese slices. Remind children that to be a square, all the sides must be the same length.

VOCABULARY: circle, square, side, vertex, vertices

TRIANGLES

Look at these shapes.

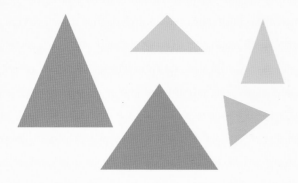

These shapes are called **triangles**.
How many sides does a triangle have?
How many vertices?

RECTANGLES

A **rectangle** is a shape that is similar to a square.

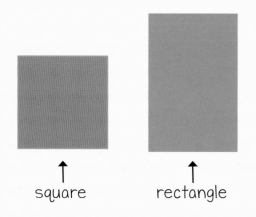

square   rectangle

TRY THIS:

Look around you.
Can you find some objects
that are shaped like a triangle?

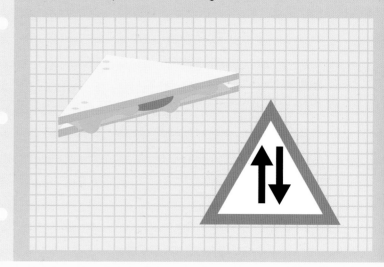

What is the same about
a square and a rectangle?
What is different?

TRY THIS:

These shapes are all rectangles. They all have 4 vertices.
They all have 2 long sides and 2 short sides. The purple rectangle is long and thin.
Can you describe the other rectangles? Use words such as long, short, tall, fat and thin.

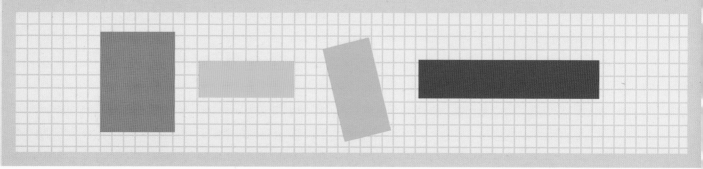

VOCABULARY: triangle, rectangle

WHICH SHAPE?

Can you remember the names of shapes?

Let's have some fun looking at shapes!

Which object is shaped like a circle?

Which object is shaped like a rectangle?

Which object is shaped like a square?

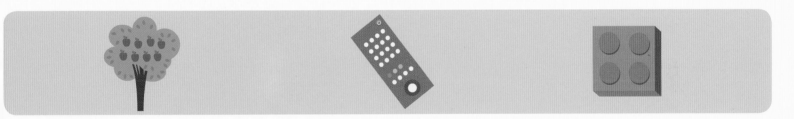

Which object is shaped like a triangle?

PARENT AND TEACHER GUIDANCE

● When you are exploring shapes with children, ask questions to lead them to discover that both triangles and rectangles may vary in shape, while circles and squares only vary in size. For example, say, "In this triangle, the sides are all the same length. Do you think the sides are the same length in that triangle?"

LINES

When you put a pencil on a piece of paper and make a long, thin mark, it is called a **line**.

Use a sharp pencil to draw clear lines.

When we draw a square, we draw lines to show the shape.

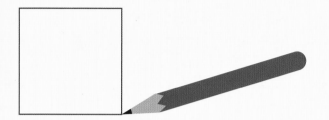

We use lines to draw triangles, rectangles and circles too.

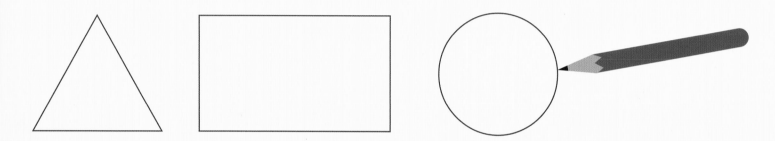

The lines below are **straight**. Which shapes have straight lines?

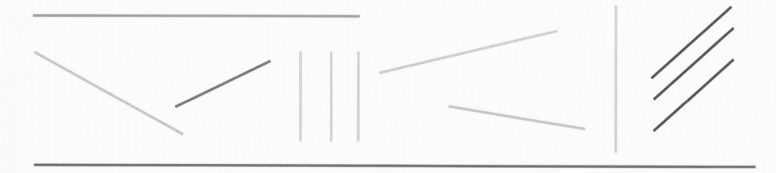

The lines below are **curved**. Which shapes have curved lines?

VOCABULARY: line, straight, curved

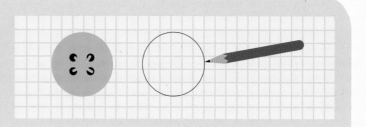

SHAPE SEARCH

There are lots of shapes in this picture. How many can you find?

Can you find a straight line?
Can you find a curved line?

How many circles can you find?
How many squares can you find?
How many rectangles can you find?
How many triangles can you find?

We have been learning about **flat** shapes.
Flat shapes are sometimes called **2D** shapes.
2D is short for two-dimensional.

Can you remember the names of all the flat shapes here?

These shapes are all flat.

You can draw them but you can't pick them up.

Let's think about some shapes you can pick up.
Here is a picture of a box.

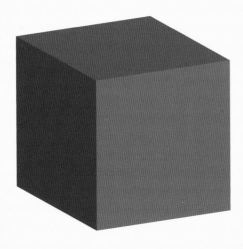

The shape of this box is a **cube**.
A cube is a shape you can pick up.
A cube is a **solid** shape.

Solid shapes are sometimes called **3D** shapes.
3D is short for three-dimensional.
You can hold a solid shape in your hand.

LENGTH, WIDTH AND HEIGHT

Hold a 3D shape in your hand.
You can measure a 3D shape in 3 ways.
You can measure its **length**, its **width** and its **height**.

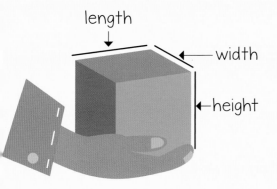

Look at these pictures of 3D objects. All these objects have length, width and height.

SOLID OR FLAT?

Look at these shapes. Which shapes look solid? Which shapes look flat?

VOCABULARY: length, width, height

LOOKING AT 3D SHAPES

You have seen this 3D shape before.
Can you remember what it is called?

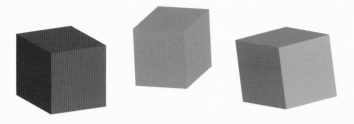

It is a cube.

Find something shaped like a cube.
Hold it in your hand and look at it.
Can you describe it?

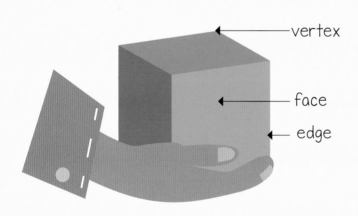

vertex

face

edge

Remember that 3D shapes are solid. Solid means that they have length, width and height. 2D shapes are flat.

Each surface of a 3D shape is called a **face**.
How many faces does the cube have?
What shape is each face?

The faces of a 3D shape meet at an **edge**.
How many edges does the cube have?

The edges of a 3D shape meet at a vertex.
How many vertices does the cube have?

A die is the same shape as a cube.

Look around.
Can you find any other objects that are cubes?
What is the same about all of them?

VOCABULARY: face, edge

CUBOID

A **cuboid** is similar to a cube.
Can you see what is the same?
Can you see what is different?

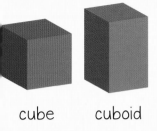

cube   cuboid

SPHERE

This shape is called a **sphere**.
A sphere is the same shape as a ball.

Find a ball and look at it.
Can you find any edges?
Can you find any vertices?
How many faces does a sphere have?

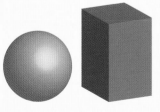

Look at the face of a sphere.
Now look at the face of a cuboid.
The sphere has a curved face.
The cuboid's faces are flat.

TRY THIS:

Look at these cuboids. Are they all the same? Can you describe how each of them is different?

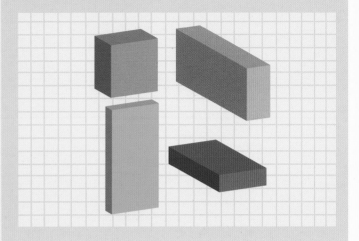

Look around for cuboids and spheres. Can you find more cuboids or more spheres?

VOCABULARY: cuboid, sphere

CYLINDER

This 3D shape is called a **cylinder**.

The flat faces of a cylinder are like a 2D shape you know. What shape are they?

Can you think of anything that is the same shape as a cylinder?
You might find something in a kitchen. How many faces does a cylinder have?

CONE

This 3D shape is called a **cone**.
Its flat face is a circle.

Ice cream sometimes comes in an object which is similar to a cone.

TRY THIS:
What 3D shapes are these objects similar to?

CEREAL

SOUP

PARENT AND TEACHER GUIDANCE
● Children can explore the shapes of the faces of 3D shapes by pressing them into wet sand or modelling clay.

VOCABULARY: cylinder, cone

MAKE 3D SHAPES

Use playdough to make different 3D shapes.

YOU WILL NEED:

- 3D shape models
- playdough
- a ruler
- a plastic knife

Let's have some fun making shapes!

1 First, try making a cylinder. Look at a cylinder model and think about its shape. You will need to make a curved face and 2 flat faces.

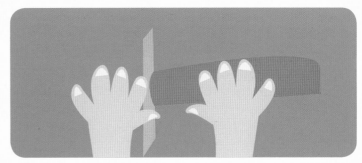

3 Press the ends flat with a ruler or cut them carefully with a plastic knife.

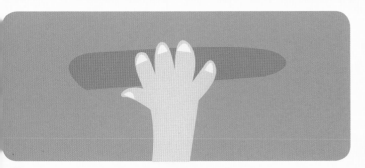

2 Roll a piece of playdough into the shape of a sausage with your hand.

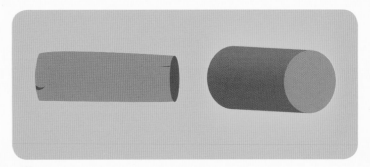

4 Display your shape next to the 3D model. Now try making some other 3D shapes.

PARENT AND TEACHER GUIDANCE

- Children's playdough 3D shapes will not be accurate, but will make them look carefully at the shape of the 3D models.

Let's look at patterns!

When things are arranged in an **order**, we call it a **pattern**.

Look at the shapes.

What does the first shape look like?
The first shape is an orange circle.

What comes next in the pattern?
A green circle comes next.

Move your finger along the line and say what colour each circle is.

What do you notice about the order of the colours?
The first 2 shapes are an orange circle and a green circle.
Then the shapes continue in this order to the end of the line.

TRY THIS:

Can you describe the order of the objects in the patterns below?

TRY THIS:

Use two colours of beads to make a bead pattern like this.
Which colour bead will you put on first?
Which colour will you use next?
Can you explain how you will continue the pattern?

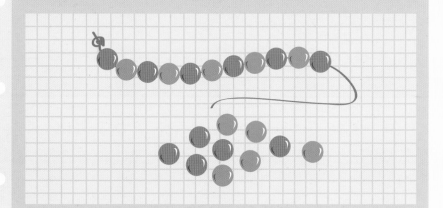

CONTINUE THE PATTERN

Look at the patterns below.
What comes next in each pattern?

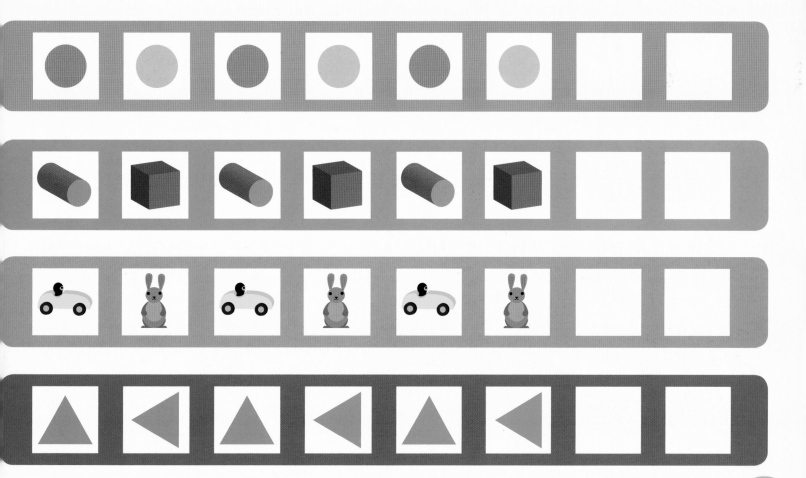

Look around you. Can you find any patterns of shapes or objects?

A STEP FURTHER

Let's think about some patterns with more shapes in them.

Look at these shapes.

Move your finger along the line, naming each shape. Can you see the pattern?
The pattern is triangle, circle, square.

WHAT COMES NEXT?

Look at the patterns below. Describe each pattern. Then say what comes next.

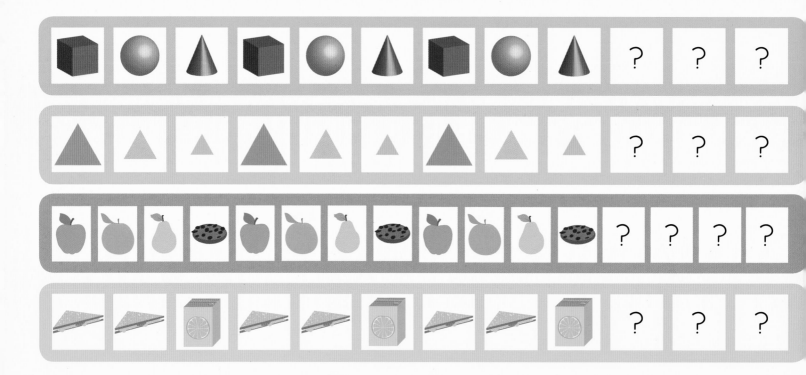

TRY THIS:
Draw these shapes and then repeat them to make a pattern.

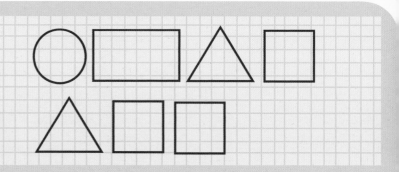

PRINTING PATTERNS

You can make colourful printed patterns with fruit and vegetables.

1 Ask an adult to cut some fruit and vegetables.

2 Dip the flat side of a piece of fruit or vegetable into some paint.

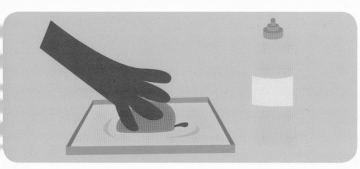

3 Start at one edge of the paper. Press the painted side onto the paper.

4 Lift it off carefully to see the print you have made.

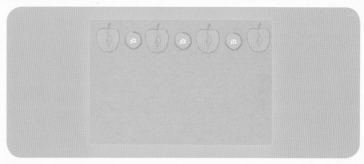

5 Now print a different item. Repeat these 2 prints to make a pattern.

6 When you have finished the row, make more patterns underneath.

You can use different objects to print with. Try using plastic shapes or cookie cutters.

When we describe where something is, we are talking about its **position**.

Can you use position words to describe where I am on this page?

Look at the picture.

The fork is **next to** the plate.
The knife is **beside** the plate.
The plate is **between** the fork and the knife.

Can you think of some other ways to describe how the objects are arranged?
The fork is **left** of the plate.
The knife is **right** of the plate.

Look at this picture.

Is the butterfly on the left or the right of the flower?
Is the bee on the left or the right?

PARENT AND TEACHER GUIDANCE

● There is a lot of vocabulary associated with position. Help children understand position words while they perform everyday activities. For example, stress the position words when you ask children to help lay the table, saying, "Put the fork on the left of the plate," "Put the cup near the knife."

CUBES IN A ROW

Look at the line of coloured cubes below.

How many colours can you see?

Answer the questions about the position of each cube.

Which cube is next to the blue cube?

Which cube is between the yellow cube and the red cube?

Which cube is to the left of the purple cube?

Which cube is to the right of the red cube?

TRY THIS:

Follow these instructions to draw a line of shapes. Start by drawing a yellow circle.

1. Draw a green star to the left of the yellow circle.

3. Draw a red triangle next to the star.

2. Draw a blue square next to the circle.

4. Draw a purple circle to the right of the square.

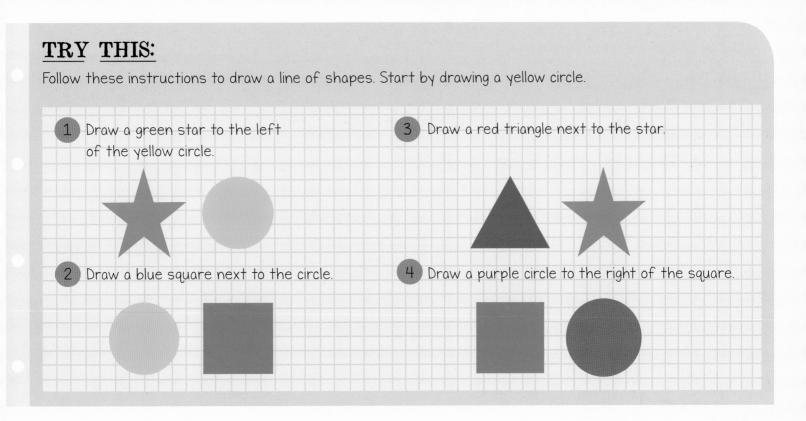

PARENT AND TEACHER GUIDANCE

- Have children draw or position objects such as cubes or toys following your instructions.
- Arrange some objects and ask questions about their position.

BIRDS IN THE TREE

Let's look at some more positions.
Read the labels and point to each bird.

How many birds can you see in the tree?

The orange bird is at the **top** of the tree.

The orange bird is **above** the blue birds.

Three blue birds are in the **middle** of the tree.

The blue birds are **below** the orange bird.

The white bird is at the **bottom** of the tree.

The white bird is **under** the blue birds.

Where is the pink bird? Use position words to explain.
Where is the yellow bird? Use position words to explain.
Can you think of any other position words you could use to describe the birds?

VOCABULARY: top, middle, bottom, above, below, under

BREAKFAST TIME

Look at the picture.
Read the labels and point to each object.

PARENT AND TEACHER GUIDANCE

● Children often find 2D representations of position confusing, particularly when thinking about in front of and behind, above and below. Use materials such as bricks and toys to reinforce their learning about position.

The cereal is **behind** the milk.

Some of the strawberries are **out** of the box.

The butter is **close** to the cereal.

CEREAL

The jam is **far** from the butter.

BUTTER

JAM

The milk is **near** the bowl.

The spoon is **in** the bowl.

TRY THIS:

Look at how the cubes are arranged below on the grid. Use the position words you have learnt to say where each cube is.

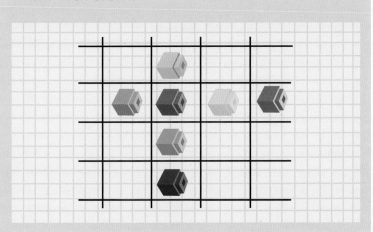

Try laying out some cubes or counters, and ask a friend to describe their position.

VOCABULARY: behind, close, out, far, near, in

23

Let's practise using position words.
You will need a friend to play this game with.

Here's a game for you to play outside in a playground.

Go to the top of the climbing frame.

1 Use the position words you know to tell your friend where to go.

Go in the playhouse.

3 Take turns giving instructions.

I'm at the top of the climbing frame.

2 Now ask your friend to describe her position.

How many position words can you use?

I'm in the playhouse.

4 Now describe your position.

PARENT AND TEACHER GUIDANCE

● Play this game anywhere children can move around and climb, such as during PE lessons or on play equipment at home.

● On a smaller scale, place a hula hoop on the ground, or make a circle with chalk or a rope. Give children instructions such as, "Stand in the hoop," "Go in front of the hoop."

LET'S DRAW

Follow the instructions to make a picture.

YOU WILL NEED:
- a large sheet of paper
- crayons or coloured pencils

1 Draw the sun at the top of the paper on the right.

2 Draw a tree in the middle of the paper.

3 Draw some flowers next to the tree.

4 Draw a bird on the tree.

5 Draw another bird next to the first one.

6 Draw a cloud near the tree.

7 Draw a girl and a boy to the right of the tree.

Add some more objects to your picture. Say where they are in the picture.

25

When we talk about the way a person or thing's position changes, we are talking about **movement.**

Look around you. Can you see anything moving?

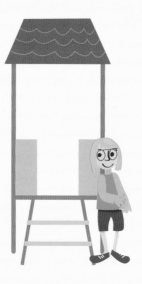

The girl is **inside** the playhouse.

The girl is **outside** the playhouse.

The girl has moved from inside the playhouse to outside the playhouse.

Things can move in different ways.

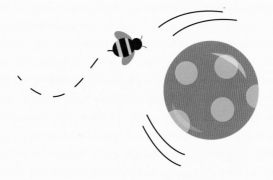

This snail is moving slowly.

This bee is flying.

This ball is rolling.

This rabbit is hopping.

This boy is running fast.

Can you think of any other ways things can move?

VOCABULARY: movement, inside, outside

When we talk about the path that something moves along, we are talking about **direction**.

forwards

backwards

This swing is moving. It is moving **forwards** and **backwards**. Forwards and backwards are directions.

Can you think of any other direction words?

Up
the ladder.

Down
the slide.

Left to
the café.

Right to the
playground.

TRY THIS:

Move toy cars around on a playmat or toy trains on a track. As you move them, say how they are moving and which direction they are moving in.

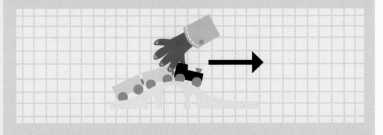

The train goes over the bridge forwards.

PARENT AND TEACHER GUIDANCE

- Encourage children to think of different ways things can move, such as sliding, jumping and crawling. You can play a game using different direction and movement vocabulary, for example, "Crawl forwards," "Roll backwards."

- Ask children to make radio-controlled toys, such as cars, move in a particular direction or speed.

VOCABULARY: direction, forwards, backwards, up, down

Here's a game you can play with a friend to help you learn more about directions. You'll need to find a big space to play it in.

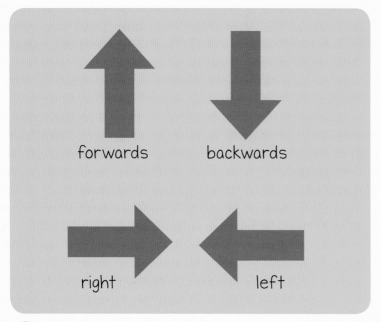

1 Carefully copy the arrows and the words onto both sheets of paper. Give one copy to your friend.

3 Ask your friend to describe where they are.

2 Start by telling your friend which way to go.

4 Take turns at giving instructions.

CARROT GAME

Help the rabbit find all the carrots and get home.

Can you remember which way is left and which way is right? Look at page 20 if you have forgotten.

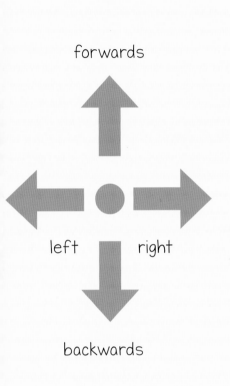

forwards

left   right

backwards

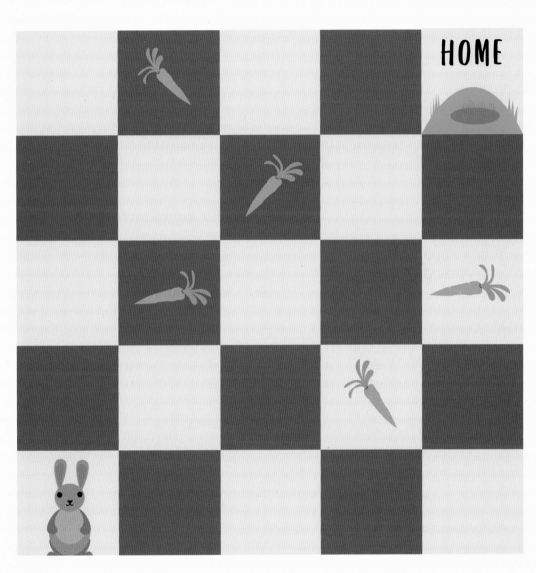

HOME

1. Start by putting your finger on the square with the rabbit. Move your finger right 3 squares. Move your finger forwards 1 square. You have reached the first carrot.

2. Move around the board to reach all the carrots. Say which direction you are moving in and how far each time.

3. When you have passed all the carrots, say how the rabbit will get home.

PARENT AND TEACHER GUIDANCE

- Make a grid on a large sheet of paper and have children draw different places in the squares, for example shops, cinema, library, school, swimming pool. Have them take turns to direct each other to different sites on the grid.

TURNING

Let's learn about **turning**. You will need to find a clear space you can easily turn around in.

Don't turn around too fast or you might fall over!

1. Put your feet together. Put your arm straight out in front of you.

2. Turn around on the spot until you are facing the same way again. The arrow shows how you have turned. You have turned all the way round. We call this a **whole turn**.

3. Now turn around half way. We call this a **half turn**.

4. Face the way you started again. Now turn so you are facing right. You have made a **quarter turn**.

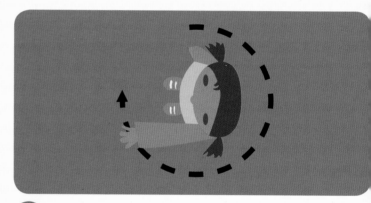

5. Face the way you started again. Make a quarter turn. Turn one more quarter turn. Turn another quarter turn. You have made a **three-quarter turn**.

PARENT AND TEACHER GUIDANCE

● Children need plenty of opportunities to turn themselves before they can apply this concept to other things.

VOCABULARY: turning, whole turn, half turn, quarter turn, three-quarter turn

DIFFERENT DIRECTIONS

Before you start to turn, you have to choose which direction to turn.

You can turn to the right.

You can turn to the left.

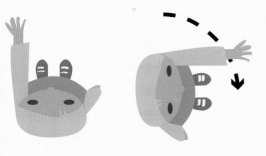

quarter turn to the right

half turn to the left

CLOCKWISE

How do the hands of a clock turn?
Look at the big hand. When the clock shows
o'clock, the big hand points straight up.

The big hand makes a half turn to the right
to reach **half past**.
A turn to the right is called a **clockwise** turn.
Clockwise means the same direction that a
clock's hands turn.

What sort of turn does the big hand
make to show that an hour has passed?

VOCABULARY: o'clock, half past, clockwise

TOOLS FOR SUCCESS

Most of the maths activities in the book can be carried out using everyday items, but the following mathematical tools are used in this book and you may find them useful.

2D shape templates
Children are likely to find drawing shapes difficult. Using 2D shape templates to draw around allows them to create shapes more quickly and easily.

2D sticky shapes
2D sticky shapes enable children to use shapes for making pictures and patterns without having to draw the same shape many times.

3D shape models
3D shape models in different sizes can help children to explore the properties of shapes. They are particularly important as flat images of 3D shapes such as those in this book can be difficult for young children to understand.

Beads and strings
Coloured beads that can be threaded onto strings are a good tool for children to begin making and understanding simple repeating patterns.

Clock
An analogue clock can be used to demonstrate quarter, half and whole turns, as well as left and right turns.